Sculptures of Cats

In Russia and around the World

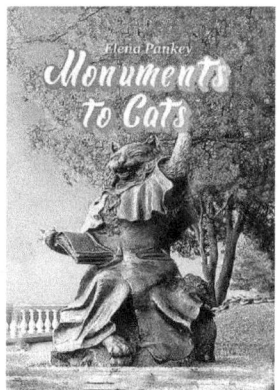 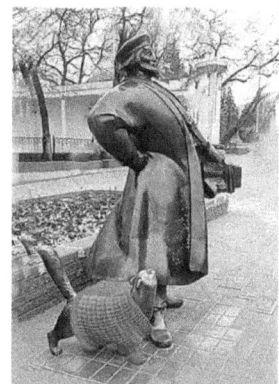 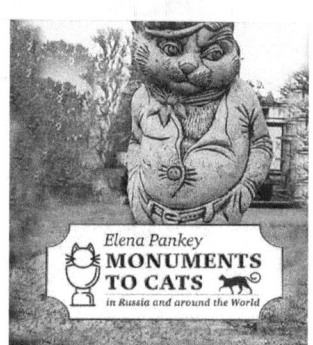

Title ID: 7661740

ISBN-13: 978-1978025851 AND ISBN-10:1978025858

By Elena Pankey

Sculptures of Cats in Russia and World

Contents

About Cats	3
Taming	6
Did You Know…	7
Interesting Tributes	11
Koroviev and Behemoth	15
Cat of Gelendzhik	18
Kitten from Lizyukov Street	20
Cats of St.Petersburg	21
Cat Totti	27
Cat of Kazan	28
Ukrainian Cats	29
Bench of Reconciliation	31
Cats of England	33
Cat Towser	36
Whittington's Cat	38
Bremen Town Musicians	40
Homeless Cats	41
A million dollars cat	42
Around the Globe	43
Our Wonderful Cats	45
About Author	48

About Cats

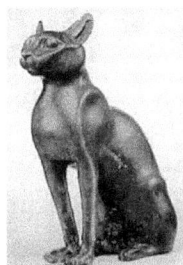

In Russian language, the word cat means either a representative of the biological subspecies regardless of gender, or the female of this subspecies. At present, there are about 600 million domestic cats and about 200 breeds in the world. The different breeds go from long-haired (Persian) to woolless (sphinx) breeds.

According to the Jewish legend, Noah prayed to God, asking to protect the food on the ark from the rats. In response, God made the lion sneeze, and a cat jumped out of it.

The first monuments of cats are known since time immemorial.

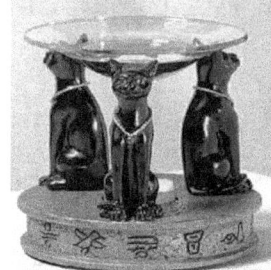

Basically, these are sculptures found in Egypt. For example, in the zoological garden of Memphis there is a statue of the ancient Greek goddess Sekhmet with several cats at her feet. Among the bas-reliefs with images of ancient Sumerian kings there is also one where the ruler holds a cat in his arms.

Domestication of the cat occurred in the Middle East, where the ancient human civilizations were born. This happened when a person moved to a settled way of life. At the development of agriculture, it became necessary to preserve surplus food from rodents. For example, the remnants of the once powerful fortress of Teixe

Baini were discovered in Armenia, which ended the existence in the 6th century BC. And during the archaeological excavations in Cyprus

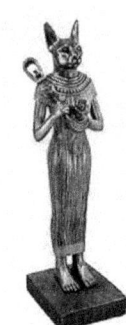

was found a joint burial of a man and a cat, which dates back to 7500 BC. There is a legend in which it is told how the Egyptians lost the battle to the Persians because of cats. The cult of cats in Egypt existed almost to our days. And in ancient Egypt, the cat was revered as a sacred animal.

Another legend is telling that the storehouses of the pharaoh with the grain were invaded by a huge number of rodents. The cats of the pharaoh could not cope with such an army of pests-rodents. Then Pharaoh ordered to collect all cats from his subjects and put them in storage with grain. But the subordinates did not want to give their cats to Pharaoh. Then, the priests went to stealth and declared cats as sacred animals. This meant that the cat was equated with a deity (as well as the Pharaoh). The ordinary people could no longer have cats or even touch them, but only Pharaoh could own cats.

Ancient Egyptian goddess Bast (Bastet) - the goddess of fertility - was portrayed with the cat's head and was the patroness of love. In addition, it served as a symbol of the Sun and Moon, was the patroness of the souls of the dead in the afterlife, was responsible for the fertility of animals and people. Such a variety of "duties" was common for the ancient Egyptian deities. Some of the wonderful works of ancient masters of Egypt came up to our time to speak about the worship of a cat.

Despite the fact that cats have been domesticated long enough, most cats are able to survive in conditions of being outside of human habitation. But they quickly become wild again. Untamed cats often live solitary and hunt alone, but sometimes they form small colonies of several females with kittens.

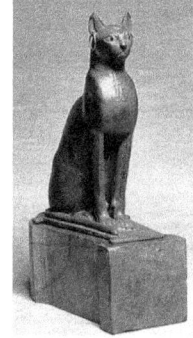

Our beloved animals were often immortalized in sculptures and paintings, honors were honored as a deity. For the harm done to the cats, the perpetrator was severely punished, and for the murder of the animal he was sentenced to death. There were special cat's cemeteries, where animals were buried with great honors. The owner wore mourning for several days and shaved his eyebrows as a sign of great sadness to the deceased cat. The cats were embalmed and placed in a family tomb or animal cemetery with tiny mummies of mice. The smuggling of cats from ancient Egypt was punishable by death. In 1860 in Egypt, near the city of Beni-Hassan, archeologies found a cat's cemetery. And in 1890, during excavations of the ancient city of Bubastis, it was found more than three hundred cat mummies. Currently, cats are one of the most popular pets and in the world they have set a lot of statues.

Taming

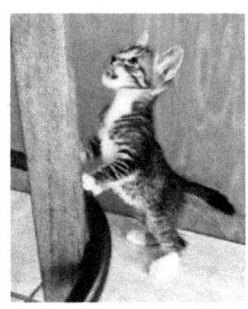
Tamed cats began to spread from Africa around the world. This was largely promoted by sea voyages, when people took cats with them to ships to protect food supplies from rats. In Greece, the animals have bred and become very popular. The cat is a beautiful and graceful animal, and Greeks appreciated beauty in all. Cats began to use instead of weasels and ferrets, which were used previously to combat rodents. With the development of trade relations between Europe and Asia, cats will gradually settle the countries of the East. Here, the cat is treated differently than in the West. In addition to its usual function
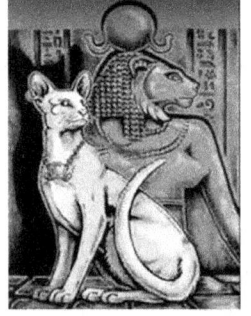
of protecting the crop from pests, the cat is something like a living mascot guarding the master and his house from evil spirits and bringing happiness and well-being. It was believed that with age, the cat's mystical qualities intensified and the older a cat, the more happiness it brings.

The cat was not the object of worship in the countries of the East, as in ancient Egypt, but was revered and respected. Then, in our time, a cat is considered the embodiment of coziness and well-being in the house, the protection of its owners from all sorts of scourges and evil forces.

Did You Know…

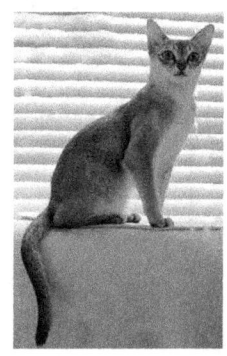

The smallest cat in the world is the Singaporean. On the bank of the Singapore River there is a cat-like monument, the prototype cat was considered the mascot of the country and it was called Kunsita. The short-haired cats of Singapore, derived from aboriginal cats, were taken out of the country in 1975. These small animals have a rare color, the cat-mail weighs about 3 kg and the cat-female weighs about 2 kg. The brown hairs are vividly highlighted in the background called "warm old ivory." But those very small cats have not been found in Singapore for the last 30 years. The representatives of the Singaporean are very timid, usually hide in ditches and a trumpet. The smallest wildcat for today is the Blackfoot Cat, whose females are less

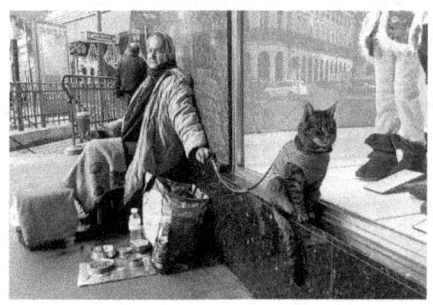

than 50 cm in length and can weigh only 1.2 kg. The largest wild cat is the Amur Tiger. It can grow up to 3.6 m in length (like a small car) and weigh up to 320 kg.

It is interesting that cats, like horses, sometimes move in amble. In America, cats are celebrated with the help of feline races. In the city of Little Rock, cats are run annually at a 150-meter distance, and the winner in the race receives the main prize - $ 2,000.

Some Siamese cats mow through the eyes due to a special device of the eye nerves. The cat has about 12 mustaches on each side 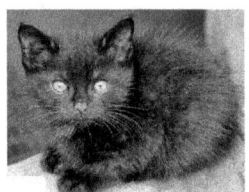 of the muzzle. The most expensive cat in the world named Little Nicky cost its owner $ 50,000. She is a clone of a former cat, died of old age.

In the story of the cats there were also quite scary women. In Spanish-Jewish folklore there is a parable that Adam's first wife, Lilith, turned into a black vampire cat sucking the blood of sleeping babies. Perhaps, it is this fact that led to the belief that a cat can strangle a sleeping baby or "suck" its breath.

At the time of the Spanish Inquisition, Pope Innocent VIII recognized cats as devil's assistants, and thousands of cats were burned. Unfortunately, the mass killing of cats led to a sharp increase in the population of rats, which aggravated the consequences of the "Black Death" (plague epidemic). In the Middle Ages cats were associated with black magic, and on St. John's Day people all over Europe stuffed them into sacks and threw them into bonfires. Others - sewed clothes from cat skins, where the coat took about 24 cat skins.

Until now, in many parts of the world a black cat is considered a bad sign. In America the white cats are a symbol of luck, especially a white cat on the threshold before the wedding. Domestic cats are the only kind of cat, capable of keeping the tail upright when walking. All wild cats keep their tails horizontally or between their legs when walking.

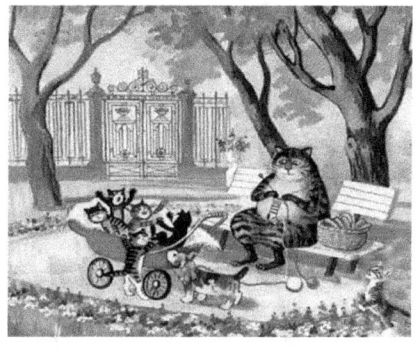

***

Cats have unigque ability: to find their way home from anywhwere. According to experts, cats either determine their location by the angle of sunlight, or cats have magnetized cells in the brain that act like a compass.

***

Wise people say: If a cat worries, rushes around the house, jumps on everything and scratches, it is to a strong wind or a hurricane. When the cat calms down, it means that the storm will soon cease.

***

If the cat thoroughly cleanses the ears, it is to the rain. In ancient Rome they said: "If the cat washes behind the ears, it means that it feels that holes appear in the sky"

***

Cats live about 15 years. If the cat is three years old, this corresponds to the age of 20 years of a person age. If a cat is 8 years old, then this is 40 years in recalculation for people years, and if the cat is 15, then we are 70 years old.

Interesting Tributes

God created cat so that the person had a tiger that can be petted (Hugo)

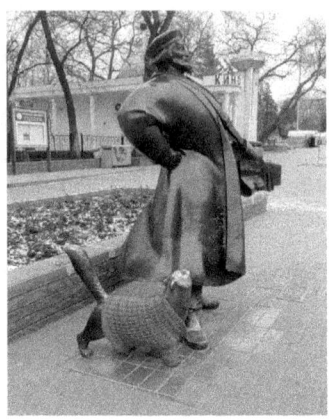 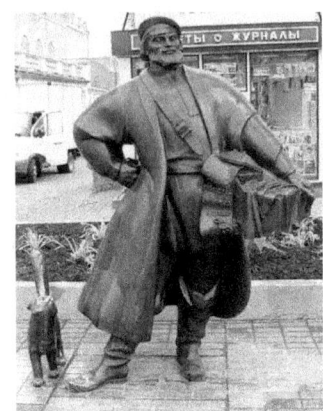

The sculptural composition "The merchant-peddler and his cat-bayun" or "The merchant with a cat" is located almost in the center of **Rostov-on-Don** (Russia), near Gorky Park, near the station, near the cafe "Golden Ear". The Man-Chapman is a symbol of a city with great trade, a merchant city. From the box hangs the letter with the inscription: "Trade righteously - in profits you will!" Local residents and tourists especially fell in love with a cat rubbing against the feet of a peddler. The cat is so often pressed that it has become shiny as a gold. People said it brings a good mood to the visitors of the monument.

***

The sages noticed that if the cat sits curled up in a bowl, it will be frost and cold.

Sculptures of Cats in Russia and World

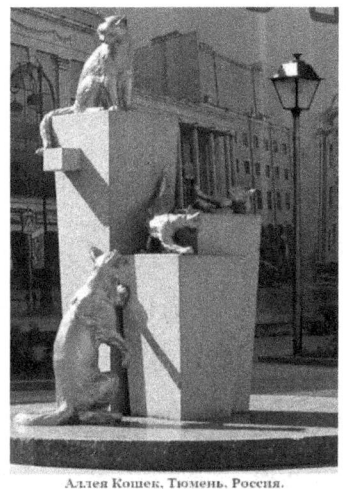
Аллея Кошек, Тюмень, Россия.

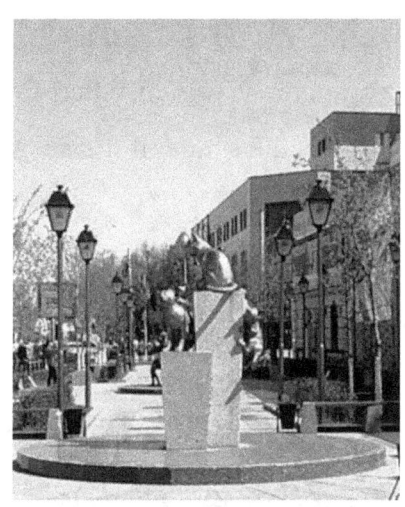

It town of **Tyumen** (Russia) one whole square has cat monuments. There are exactly 12 sculptures of cats and kittens. It cast from the iron and covered with a special gold paint. They decorate square, which is now called the "Square of Siberian cats."

***

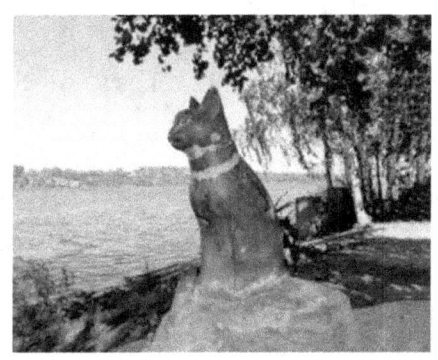

In **Ples** (Russia, Ivanovo region, Privolzhsky district), on the city dock, there is a monument to an ordinary cat that sits on a pebble and looks thoughtfully at the opening landscape. The chairman of the Community of the Plesk, artists Vitaly Panchenko had a beloved domestic cat Mucha, who died from dog bites. The artist's wife Galina wanted to perpetuate that cat and offered to make a statue. The Belarusian sculptor Oleg Illarionov often visited the area and decided to make such present tothecity. This monument was installed in 2008. Citizens and tourists enjoy to their hearts the statue of the cat Mucha.

***

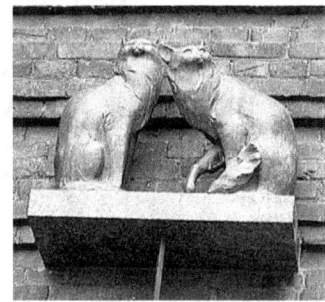

It is an interesting monument to cats located on the building of the faculty of primary classes of **Krasnoyarsk** State Pedagogical University. It symbolizes motherhood and custody of children. The cat couple appeared on the university wall in 2003, and immediately rumor spread that if a ring attached to the monument from below was tossed a coin, it would bring good luck.

***

On Volzhsky Prospect of the city of **Samara**, it is a monument

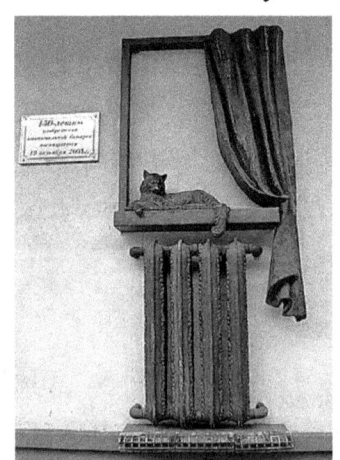

with a cat on a heating battery. It was installed to the 150th anniversary of the invention of the heating battery. It locates at the entrance of the **Samara** State Regional Power Plant. A cat sits on batteries, for which the battery is a favorite place in winter in any home. Cat's nose is very shiny from the touch for "luck" of many people, who believe in superstition.

Sculptures of Cats in Russia and World

***

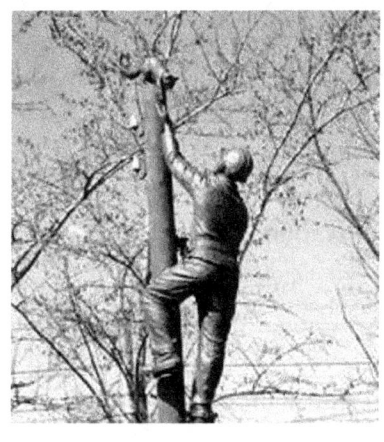

There are two funny monuments dedicated to cats in **Nizhny Novgorod.** One is called *"Cats are catching pigeons,"* and the second is *"Electrician taking a cat off the post".* The sculptor Vadim Borovy called it: "Eyes in the eyes." The monument is made of fiberglass and copper. A worker climbs up to help a cat, who stuck on the pole. The electrician draws his hand to a frightened "Murka", who afraids and does not understand that this is her savior.

***

Below - a cat monument in **Nizhny Novgorod** (Russia)

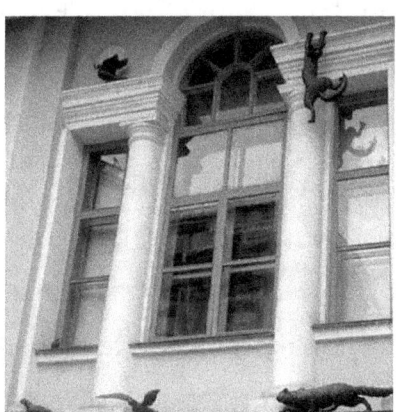
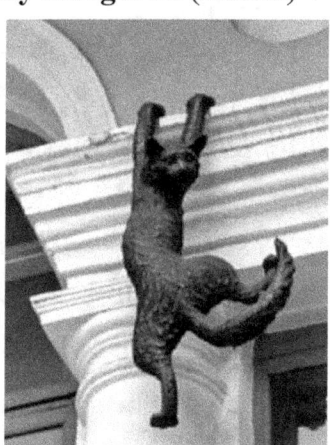

Памятник коту, Нижний Новгород, Россия.

Koroviev and Behemoth

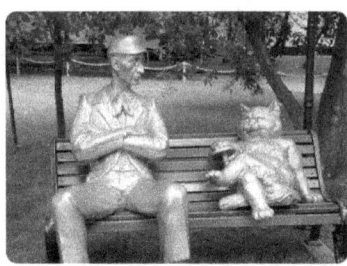

There are several monuments to cats in Moscow. There is a fun figurine of a persona-cat on the corner of Bolshoy Ovchinnikovskiy lane and Pyatnitskaya. There is a huge bronze cat has settled down at the height of the second floor and watches passers-by.

One of the most interesting is a monument to the well known cat Behemoth and Koroviev. It locates on the street of Soviet Army, house number 13. This monument by the sculptor Lyubov Mirosenko stands in one of the courtyards of the Marina Grove. It was dedicated to the famous characters of the novel by Mikhail Bulgakov "Master and Margarita".

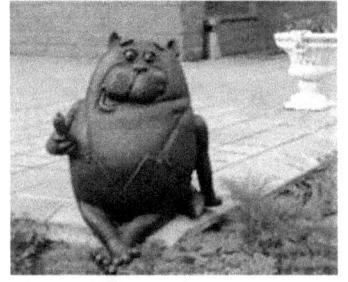

Koroviev and the cat "Hippopotamus" are sitting on a bench, conducting a leisurely conversation.

According to the testimony of the second wife of Mikhail Bulgakov, L.E. Belozerskaya, the real prototype of the Behemoth was their home favorite cat "Flushka". He was a huge gray cat. But Bulgakov made his literature cat Behemoth black. The black cats traditionally considered to be associated with evil spirits.

According to the legend, one of the "ghosts of Moscow" is a black cat. He twice a month appeared on Tverskaya Street on the odd side, between the stations

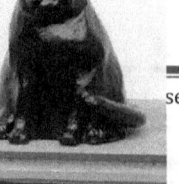

"Pushkinskaya" and "Mayakovskaya." This mysterious cat allegedly passed through the walls, appeared from nowhere, and then he quiltly disappeared. He was well-fed and educated, and brought happiness to those who saw him. Allegedly he was the prototype of the famous cat Behemoth from the "Master and Margarita". The author of the cat-sculpture on Tverskaya is Svetlana Frank.

Another monument to Koroviev and Behemoth is on Bolshaya Sadovaya street. For more than ten years these characters have sought

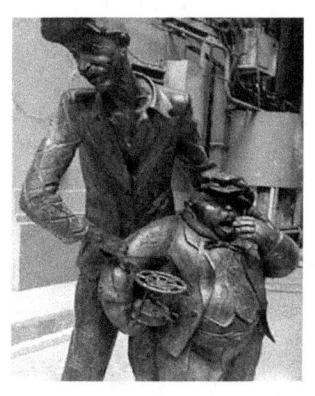

shelter. The monument also dedicated to the most charming characters of Mikhail Bulgakov's immortal novel "The Master and Margarita". The sculpture was made by Alexander Rukavishnikov in 1999. First, it was stored near the sculptor workshop in Bolshaya Molchanovk. In 2011Russia celebtated the 120th anniversary of the birth of Mikhail Bulgakov. Then, the sculptures of Fagot (Koroviev) and the cat Behemoth were installed near the Bulgakov Museum.

There is a bronze monument "Cat under the Oak" in the city of **Barnaul**. Under one bronze tree there is a bronze bench, a a bronze lonely cat is sitting there on the corner, waiting for a friend.

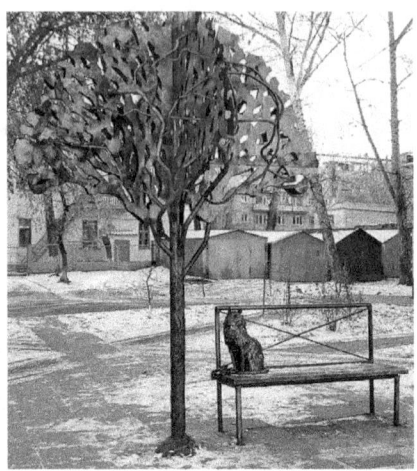

***

People say, that *"a cat has nine lives. She plays three, wanders and the other three stays in place."*

***

Some scientists believe that the most intelligent cats are from the eastern breeds, because their history has thousands of years.

***

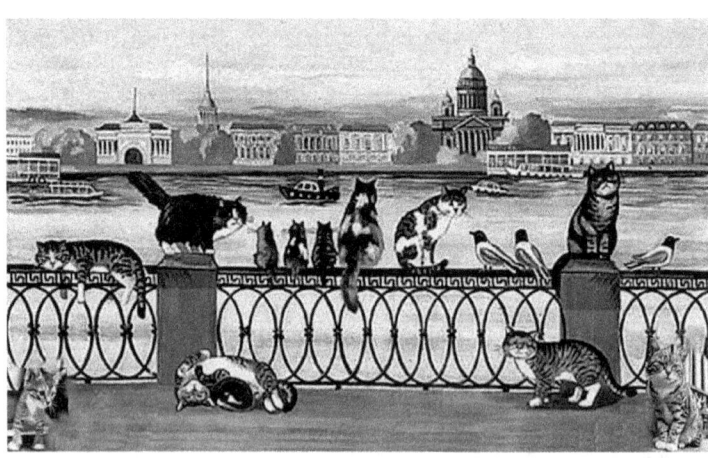

Cat of Gelendzhik

On the Black Sea, in the resort town Gelendzhik (Russia) there is a
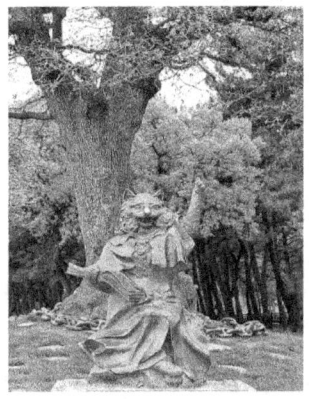
bronze monument to the scientist cat, dedicated to Alexander Pushkin's poem "Ruslan and Lyudmila." The cat stands in a robe, glasses and with a book in his paw. It turned out funny and reminds the wise scientist. His left paw is raised up in a professor's gesture, calling for silence in the audience. Cat is already shining from the frequent touches of schoolchildren, rubbing him for the luck before exams. Like in the poem, the monument stands under the spreading oak, and a huge chain lies under the tree. The best photo people get at sunset or in the morning.

The most beautiful decorative boxes are often painted with the stories
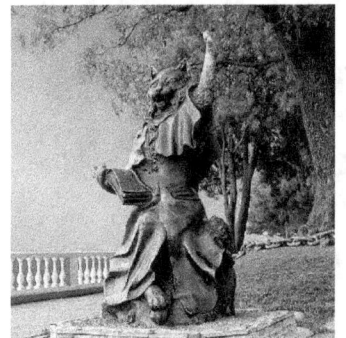
of Pushkin's fairy tales, like "Lukomore". Let us recall the great Russian poem: There're marvels there: the wood-spite roams, Midst branches shines the mermaids' tail; There are the strangest creatures' traces on the mysterious paths and moors; There stands a hut on hen's legs, hairless, without windows and doors; There visions fill a vale and forest; There, at a dawn, come waves, the coldest, on the deserted sandy shore, And

thirty knights, in armors shone, come out the clear waves in a colon, And their sea-tutor – them before; There a brave prince, in a fight, shortest, Makes to surrender a king, dread; There, to men' views, a wizard, worthless, O'er woods and seas, through clouds, aired, Carries a worrier on his beard; A princess pines away in prison, And a wolf serves her without treason; A mortar, with a witch in it, Walks as if having somewhat feet; There's King Kashchey, o'er his gold withered; There's Russian odour... Russian spirit! And I there sat: I drank sweet mead, Saw, near the sea, the green oak, growing, Under it heard a cat, much-knowing, Talking me its long stories' set. Having recalled one of its stories, I'll recite it to the world, glorious...

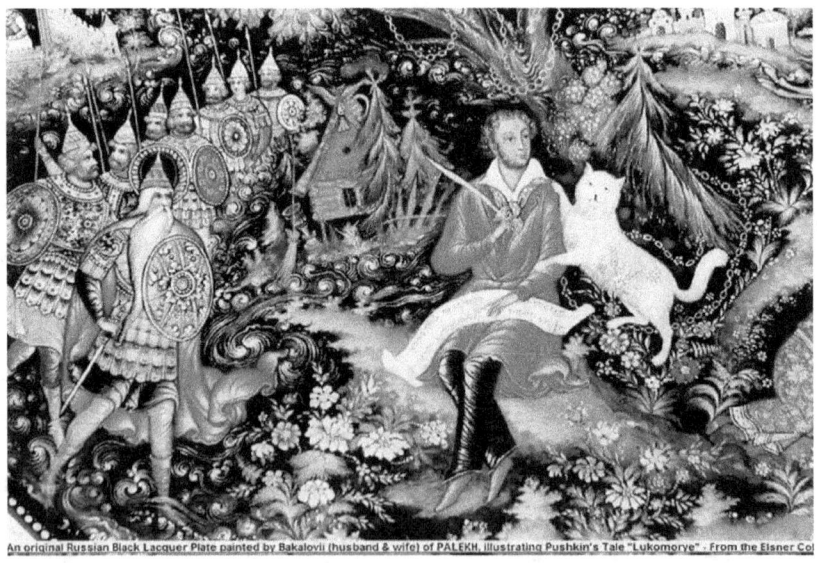

An original Russian Black Lacquer Plate painted by Bakalovii (husband & wife) of PALEKH, illustrating Pushkin's Tale "Lukomorye" - From the Elsner Col

Kitten from Lizyukov Street

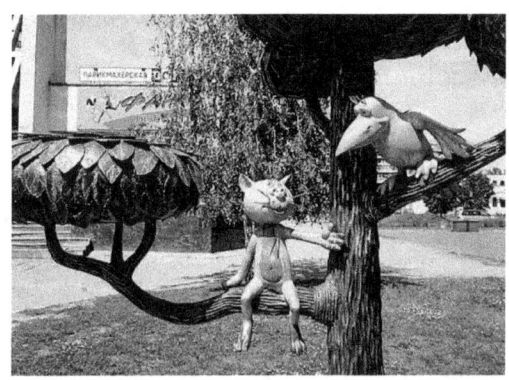

The merits of cats are beyond doubt. The monuments to dogs mostly put because of their devotion. People make the monuments to cats simply out of their love for them. For example, in **Voronezh** there is a monument to the cartoon hero, "Kitten from Lizyukov Street." First, in order to create a monument it was decided to attract the main viewers of the cartoon - children. Then, a contest was prepared in order to find the best idea for the sculptural composition. Organizers liked the most a sketch of 16-year-old schoolgirl Irina Povarova. In her drawing there was a tree with a cat and crow, sitting on it.

The creators of the monument were sculptors from Voronezh Ivan Dikunov and Elsa Pak. The monument was installed in December 2003, in the front of the entrance of the former Mir cinema, on Lizyukova Street 5. So to the nowdays, a cute kitten and another cartoon character - a crow, sit on a tree and gaily look at passers-by.

Cats of St.Petersburg

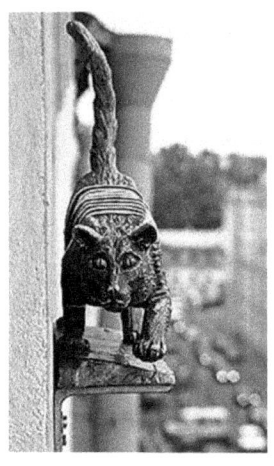

In the cat's capital of St. Petersburg are dozens of sculptural compositions with a cat. They stand in courtyards, parks and even on the eaves of houses. It was in this city that the first monument to a cat was erected.

There is a monument to a cat-character called "*Cat Matroskin*" or "*Cat in the Vest*" in St. Petersburg. The cat bent down on the facade under the window of the workshops "Mitki", the artists who invented that sculptutre.

Annually on June 8, St. Petersburg's community celebrates the most popular and truly city holiday - the World Day of Cats.

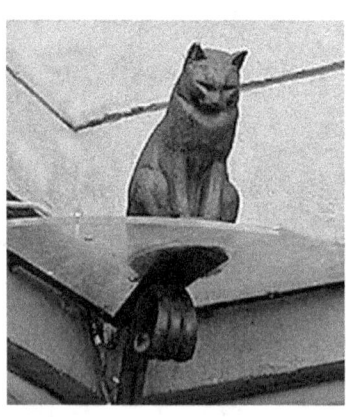 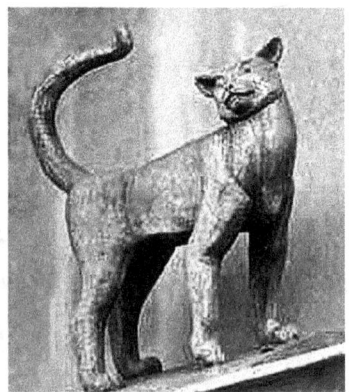

***

In the city of the Niva Rive there is another monument to a cat – to the famous "*Cat Elisha*". It locates on the building of the Eliseevskiy store on Malaya Sadovaya Street in St. Petersburg. And opposite him is settled "*Cat

Vasilisa." These two monuments are a tribute to the cats brought to Leningrad during the siege.

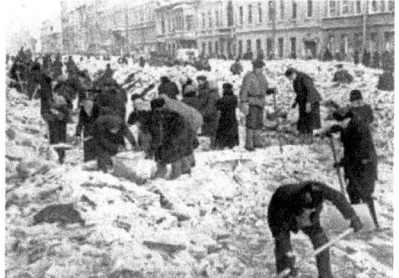 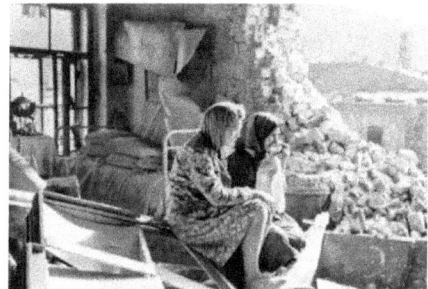

On September 8, 1941, as Adolf Hitler's forces blitzed their way into the Soviet Union during World War II. The German Army Group North laid siege to the Russian city of Leningrad (modern day St. Petersburg). The Nazis assumed the city would last mere weeks under the blockade, yet its citizens held out for nearly 900 days, enduring mass starvation, bitter cold and daily bombardments. Leningrad was finally liberated by the Soviet Red Army in January 1944, but not before a staggering 800,000 civilians had lost their lives. Hungry residents ate everything that they could find, including all cats. There was no one to protect the meager supplies of food from rodents. Then in this huge cold city swarms of rats swarmed. In April 1943, the chairman of the Leningrad City Duma issued a decree on the need to bring from Yaroslavl region and deliver to Leningrad four cars of smoky cats. According to the memoirs of a man of the blockaded city, townspeople were very happy to have the arriving purrs, and sometimes exchanged them even for the precious products.

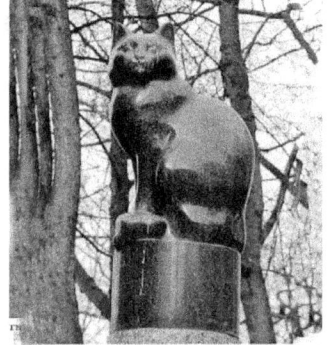

One a very touching monument to a special cat is among the famous cultural figures in the city of St. Petersburg. A granite cat the size of a meter proudly sits on a high pedestal and that special sculpture named "*Monument to the experimental cat*".

It was created thanks to the academician of the Russian Academy of Sciences Alexander Nozdrachev.

Its opening took place on November 14, 2002 on Vasilievsky Island, in the courtyard of the main building of St. Petersburg State University. The idea of creating the monument belongs to the Department of Anatomy and Physiology of St. Petersburg State

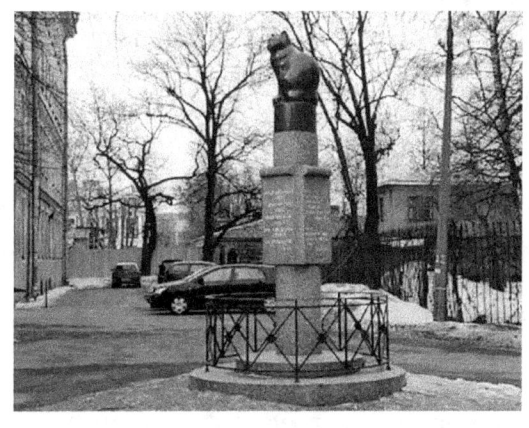

University and St. Petersburg club of cat lovers "Felis". This monument is a token of gratitude for the benefits that laboratory cats have brought to humanity. The author of the monument is the sculptor, Honored Artist of Russia, Professor Anatoly Gordeevich Dema. The architects are S. L. Mikhailov, N. N. Sokolov. The good words are knocked out on the pedestal: *"The humanity must be infinitely grateful to the cat, who*

gave the world many first-rate discoveries in physiology." This is how the academician expressed his regret about the fate of many cats, who became unknown victims of science, but thanks to which many human lives were saved.

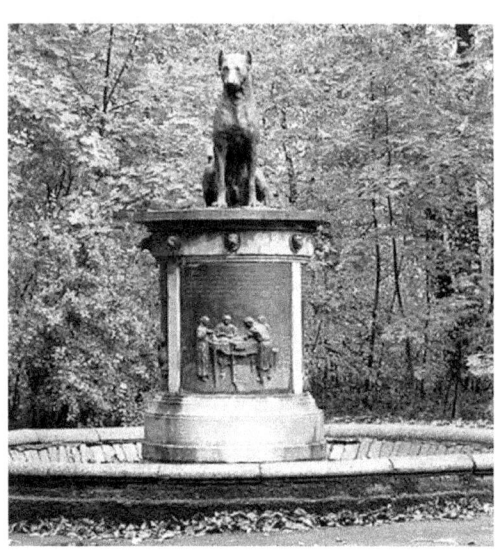

It is interesting that the concept of gratitude to dogs sacrificed to the development of science is reflected in another monument. It was installed in St. Petersburg in 1935 by the initiative of Academician Pavlov. The monument is located in the garden of the house 12 on Lopukhinskaya Street (Akademika Pavlova), on the territory of the Institute of Experimental Medicine. The scientist with the great difficulties achieved the creation of this monument. The pedestal decorated with the bas-reliefs depicting various scenes of laboratory life, and citations of the great scientist.

***

Dogs and cats always understand what do you want from them. They can even show why. They are able to feel you and know when you can approach, and when it is better to sit in a corner and not snort. With a strong desire, cats can be trained as dogs. Interestingly, than the ancient breed, the more perfected all the koshkin qualities. After all, only the best, the strongest and the cleverest cats survived, and they were able to adapt to any conditions.

***

Ivory cat sculpture in the stone is in St. Petersburg (Russia).

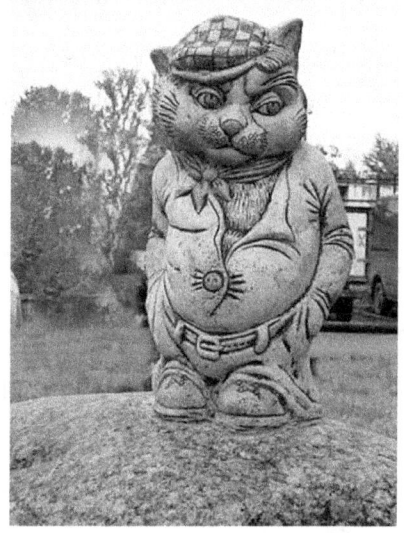

Initially, before the foundation of St. Petersburg, the island had Finnish name Kissaisaari, which meant Cat Island. To recall this, in front of the port offices of the island was set a stone sculpture of a cat.

Cat of Kanonersky island is a real hooligan boy dressed in trousers, shirt, neck scarf, hat, and boots. Monument to a Finnish cat has an address: Kanonersky Island, house 24, St. Petersburg, Russia

Cat Totti

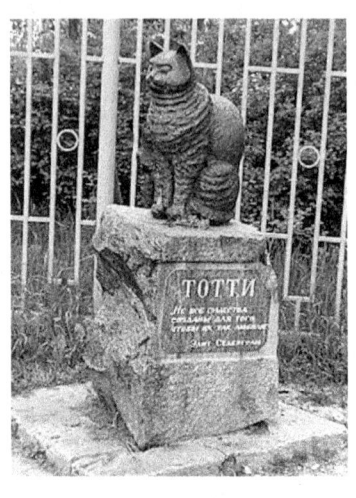

The monument to the unique cat devotion is the monument of cat Totti. It was a favorite cat of the Finnish poetess Edith Irene Södergran, who died in 1923 at the age of 31 from tuberculosis. A bronze cat sits on a granite boulder, as if he is waiting for something. The inscription reads: "*Not all beings are created to be loved so much.*" This Totti cat became a symbol of loyalty to his mistress. His bronze sculpture is known far beyond the village of Roshino, Leningrad region, where it is established. The poetess spent most of her life here in a former Finnish village. Her cat Totti (Swedish - Tutti) was answering to her love with affection and devotion. In her many photographs, Edith is imprinted with her handsome cat. But why or how the cat Totti died was not known. According to one version, mad neighbor killed him. Another version says that the faithful cat died at the grave of his mistress from the longing. Perhaps, it was this amazing and touching story that served as a reason for the Finnish sculptor Nina Terno to create a monument to the faithful Totti. Bronze Totti by the sculptor Nina Terno, appeared in the park for the poet's centenary in 1992.

Cat of Kazan

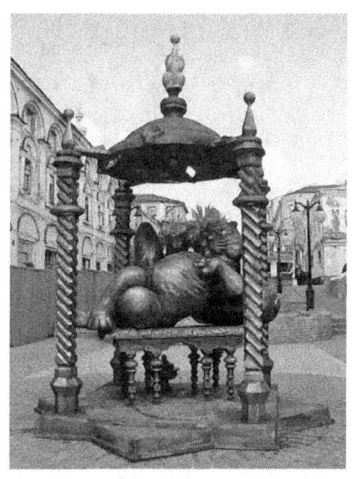

Another monument to a special cat is the so-called "*Monument to the cat Alabrysu*" or "*Cat of Kazan*". It stands in the center of **Kazan** (Republic of Tatarstan, Russia). The author of the aluminum sculpture, Igor Bashmakov, claims that he was creating a monument to an abstract cat of the Kazan breed (now extinct).

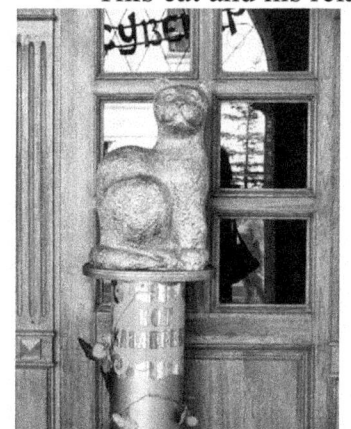

This cat and his relatives destroyed rodents so successfully that Catherine II, during her visit to Kazan was surprised by the lack of mice in the city. Having learned the reason, the empress ordered thirty of the best cats of the "Kazan breed" to send to Petersburg. Then, thoses cats were successfully fought against mice in the royal chambers.

Памятник исчезнувшей породе Казанской кошки, Казань, республика Татарстан, Россия.

Ukrainian Cats

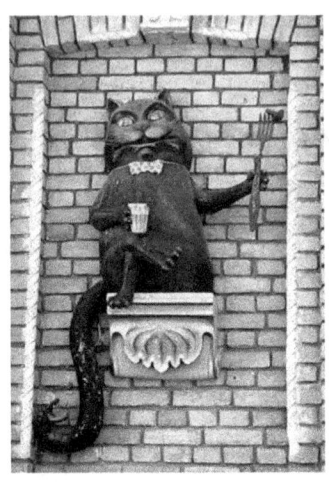

Ukraina was always as a part of the Russian Culture. Mikhail Afanasyevich Bulgakov was born May 15 in 1891 in Kiev (in the Russian Empire) and died March 10, 1940 in Moscow, the USSR. In 1909 Mikhail Bulgakov graduated from the First Kiev Gymnasium and entered the Medical Faculty of Kiev University. He was a Russian writer, playwright, theater director and actor, occultist. "Master and Margarita" was a novel that brought him world fame, and it was screened several times in Russia and in other countries.

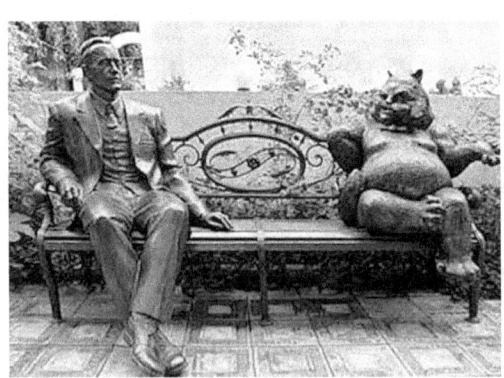

That's why a very segnifecant monument to the famous Cat Behemoth with a mushroom is staying in Kiev on the house #11 on Andreevsky descent.

Another very interesting monument under the name "*Bulgakov and the cat Behemoth on the Bench*" located in **Kharkov** (Ukraine) on the street Olminsky, house #18.

***

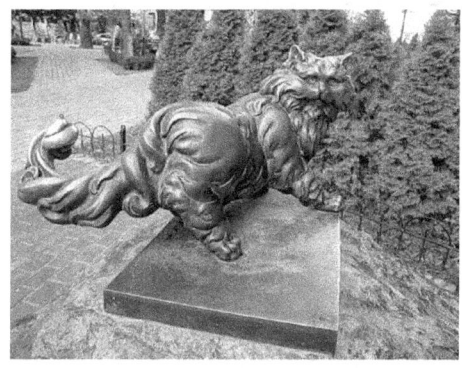

In Kiev there is an interesting bronze monument to a life-size cat - *"Cat Panteleimon"*. The prototype of the monument was the Persian cat of a smoky color. It stands near the Golden Gate. *Panteleimon* was famous for his attention to the guests of the establishment, for his kindness and gentleness. Visitors paid cat reciprocation. But one day there was a fire in the institution, and the cat died, suffocating in the smoke. Friends of the institution, saddened by his fate, gave the owners a monument, which is now popular with tourists.

***

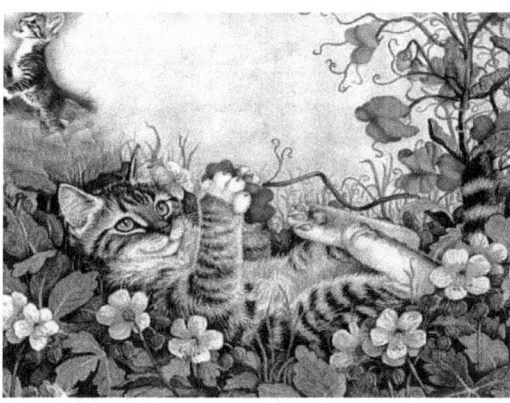

Bench of Reconciliation

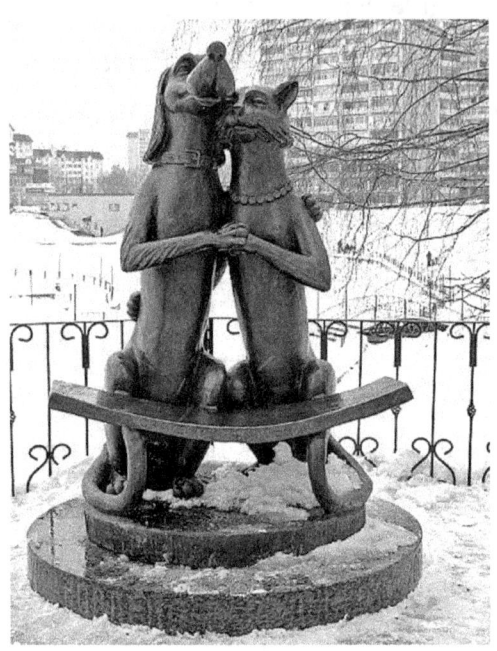

One of the most interesting monuments dedicated to the wonderful friendship between a dog and a cat is in the town of **Vidnoe** near Moscow. The monument is called *"The Bench of Reconciliation,"* because compromise is the most important for any relationships. The cat and dog were chosen as the main characters of the sculpture, but they are not depicted as two warring and irreconcilable sides. But on the contrary, they embrace each other in affection, despite the cold and snow, and smile at their friendship. These are life stories and miracles with some smart, playful cats.

***

With the help of meow, cats never communicate with each other. Their language of communication is hissing, murring and snorting. With mewing, they only address people, thinking that they speak excellently in the human language.

***

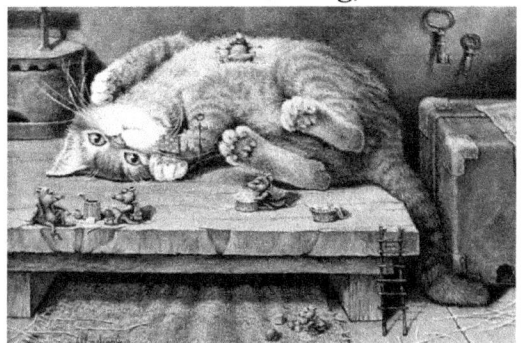

In **Yekaterinburg**, a cat named Kuzya, who protected mice, lived. His mistress found the mice in the pantry. Her cat dealt with one mouse, but regretted the four mice that hid under its thick wool. Kuzya warmed the kids and took care of them.

***

In 1963 **France** launched the first cat into the space. The French cat name was Felicette (Astrocot). Electrodes implanted in the cat's brain sent neurological signals back to Earth. Astrocot survived this flight safely.

In **China**, every resident had a statue of a cat, which in their opinion protected them from the evil spirits.

When cats appeared in **India**, they immediately became a symbol of family well-being. The goddess Sasht (the keeper of the family hearth in Hindus) looked like a cat. Hindus believed that every believer should have a cat at home or feed them.

Cats of England

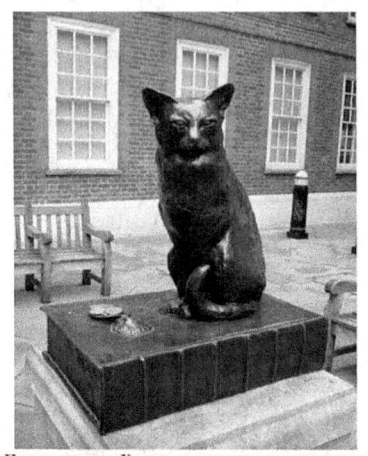

Памятник коту Ходжу, сидящему на книге своего хозяина - поэта Сэмюеля Джонсона. Адрес: Великобритания, Лондон, Gough Square неподалеку от Флит-Стрит, дом №17

Hodge was a black cat belonging to the English lexicographer Samuel Johnson of whom the writer was particularly fond.

After Hodge's death, the poet Percival Stockdale wrote "An Elegy on the Death of Dr Johnson's Favourite Cat": "Who, by his master when caressed / Warmly his gratitude expressed; / And never failed his thanks to purr / Whene'er he stroked his sable fur."

In 1997, the Mayor of London inaugurated the monument to cat Hodge, a favorite of Samuel Johnson. Dr. Samuel Johnson is a critic, scholar and poet, compiler of the explanatory English dictionary, publisher of the classic works of Shakespeare, and also a great admirer of cats. The monument to Hodge was installed near the house of Johnson, where his museum is now located. The love of the famous writer for cats was written by his friend and biographer James Boswell in the book "The Life of Samuel Johnson." There it is described that Hodge liked to sit on the table near the master, when he was working on compiling an English dictionary. And during the break from work Samuel liked to hold the cat on his hands, listening to his purr. To pamper his pet, the owner bought him oysters. The cat was so famous that the poets of that time devoted poems to the favorite Johnson. The monument is inscribed with the words "a very fine cat indeed."

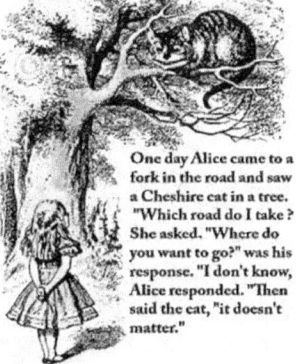 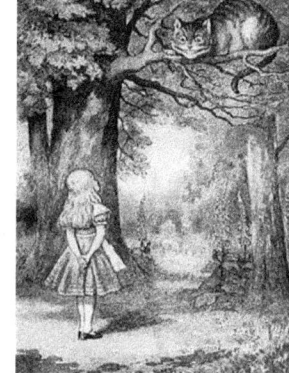

The most famous comic cat in literature is the Cheshire cat in "Alice in Wonderland" by Lewis Carroll. In the original Italian version of "Cinderella," the good fairy godmother was a cat. Due to his ability to disappear, this mysterious person personifies magic and witchcraft historically associated with cats. The Cheshire Cat is against the backdrop of the Great Orme, at the Gloddaeth Avenue road junction on West Shore. It is a wooden sculpture by Simon Hedger depicting Alice in Wonderland characters

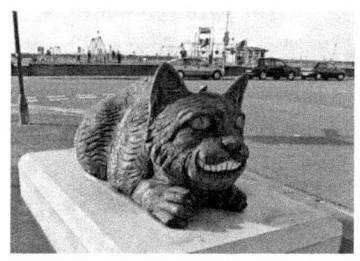

(Llandudno, Conwy, **Great Britain**). Simon Hedger has more than 25 years of experience in creating large installations. He specializes in figurative, interactive pieces. Simon's carvings are unique creations, and they are not only tell a story, but also catch the imagination of all who see them.

***

On the cat's scrotum there are receptors, when exposed to which the cat relaxes and pushes the legs to the trunk. These receptors are especially active in kittens and allow the cat-mother to move kittens from place to place.

***

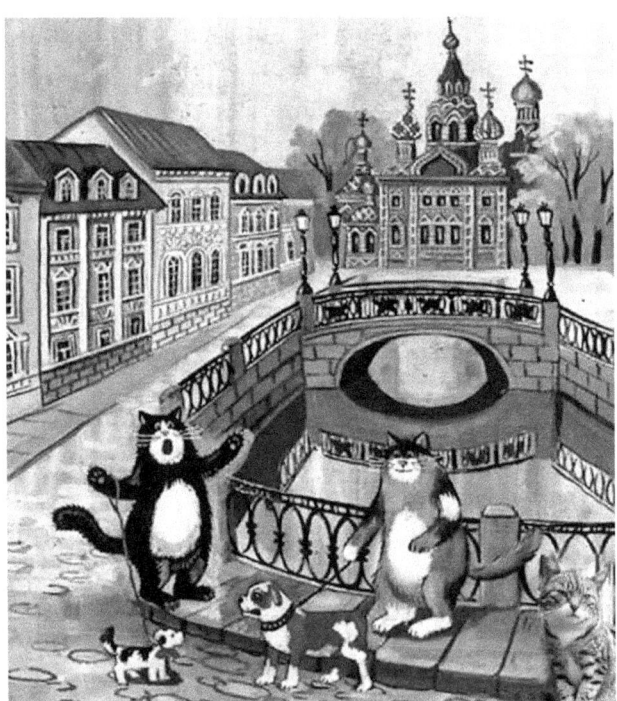

The heart of a cat beats more often than a man: up to 140 beats per minute. Favorite pastime of cats (purring) occurs about one and a half thousand times a minute.

***

It is interesting that during sleep, cats hide their claws. This applies to the whole family of felines, except for the cheeta. The cheeta claws are always ready to fight.

Cat Towser

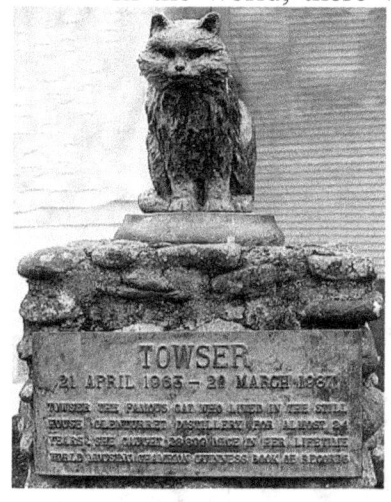

In the world, there were many monuments to dogs, for their heroism, unselfish love, devoted service, for their personal merits, and for the fact that dogs often saved people lives. But some cats also received this sign of respect.

In England, grateful descendants put a monument to a cat called Towser, who was the record holder for catching mice. In the Glenturret Whiskey cats lived from the very beginning of brewing. As is known, whiskey is driven from barley. Where the grain is, there are mice. And where the mouse - there should be a cat for balance. The cat Towser lived from 1963 to 1987, which is a very long time for a cat (equal to the human 120 years). During her long twenty-four-year life at the Glenturret Whiskey, she caught 28,899 mice. That cat was even included in the Guinness Book of Records. She brought the mouse tails to people, and it became possible to calculate her victories. Monument to cat Tauser is located at Criff, Scotland, UK.

***

If you trim the cat's mustache (vibrissae), then it will completely change in behavior. It is because with the help of a mustache they perceive the world around them. Vibrissa - long hair with supersensitive nerve endings that transmit impulses to the brain.

Some believe that vibrissae are the sixth sense of cats. Indeed, this unique mechanism allows animals to move freely in space even in total darkness. In other words, vibrissae can almost completely replace both ears and eyes.

***

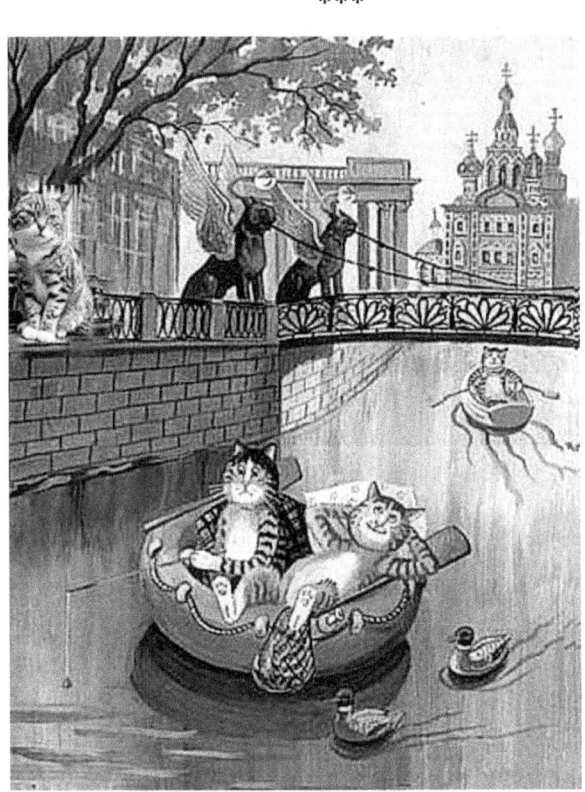

Whittington's Cat

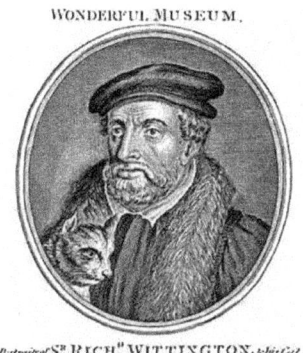

One of the most famous monuments to the legendary cats is the cat's monument to Mayor Dick Whittington, located in **London**. The cat sits on a large boulder, next to Whittington Hospital. The old tale tells that the poor orphan Dick Whittington came to London without a penny in his pocket. Then, he was hired by a wealthy merchant. Despite the prosperity in the house (or just for a reason), Dick got an "apartments" with holes in the walls. Therefore, the rats and mice lived in the house in a big amount and most of all they harassed Dick. So, as soon as Dick had money, the first thing he did was he got a cat.

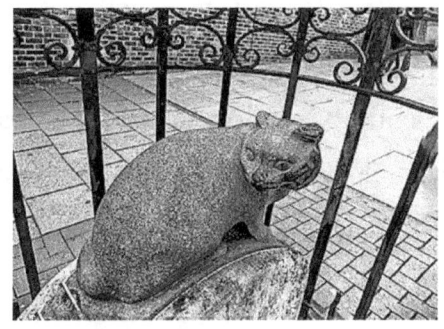

After a while, the merchant sent the ship to the shores of Africa. Traditionally, servants could try their luck in trading with the owner and send things abroad for sale. Since Dick had nothing but a cat, he gave it as a commodity. He did not believe in success, everyone joked at him, and at some point he even wanted to leave London. He reached Highgate Hill and sat down on the stone to rest, and there in the ringing of bells he heard the words: "*Oh, come back to Lon-dong. Ding-dong! Ding-dong! Lord Mayor Whittington. Ding-dong! Ding-dong!*"

Dick believed the bells and returned. Then, he learned, that his cat was profitablely sold in Africa to the Moors, suffering from the dominance of rats and mice. The merchant turned out to be an honest man and when the ship returned to England, Dick got rich. Later, he married the daughter of another merchant and became mayor of London.

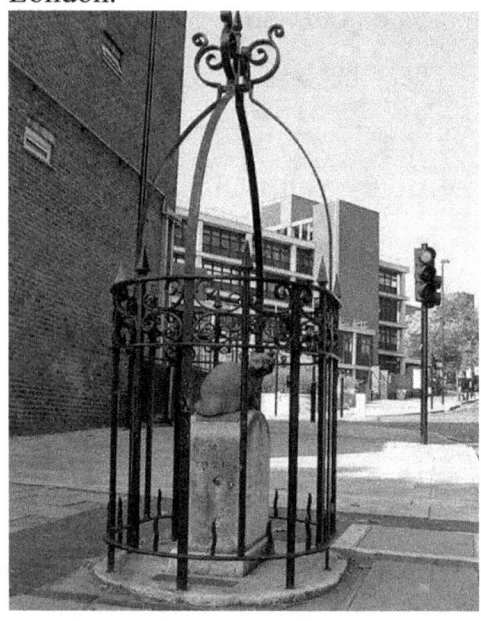

This is the story of the English fairy tale "*Whittington and his cat*" and has many variations. By the way, according to the legend, the cat sits on the same stone, where the young Dick Whittington sat down to rest and gather with thoughts. This legend is not entirely fiction, since the real Richard Whittington actually lived near by and three times became the mayor of London.

Bremen Town Musicians

In **Germany** (Bremen) is a monument to the heroes of the fairy tale of

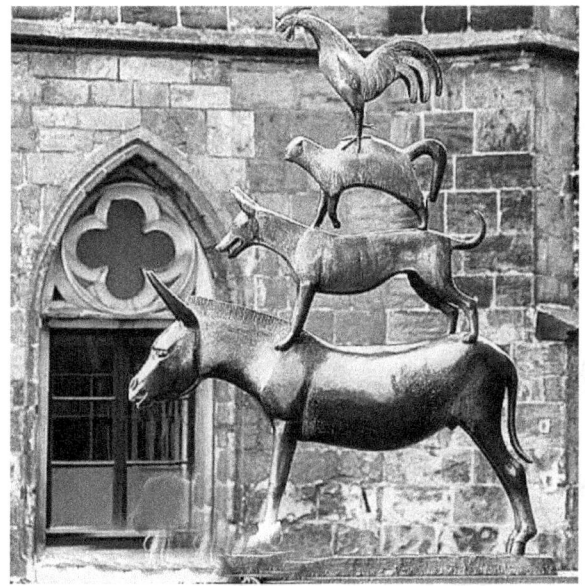

the Brothers Grimm *"Bremen Town Musicians"*. On the back of the donkey there is a dog, on it stays a cat, then on a cat stays a cock. People say, that in order to fulfill your desire, you need to hold the donkey's hoof (or two) or rub the nose of the same ass. Another joke said, that if you are a football fan and want to reinforce the confidence in the victory of your team with a pinch of magic, then be sure to tie a donkey scarf around your neck with your favorite club or national team. Laughter, yes, and only!

Homeless Cats

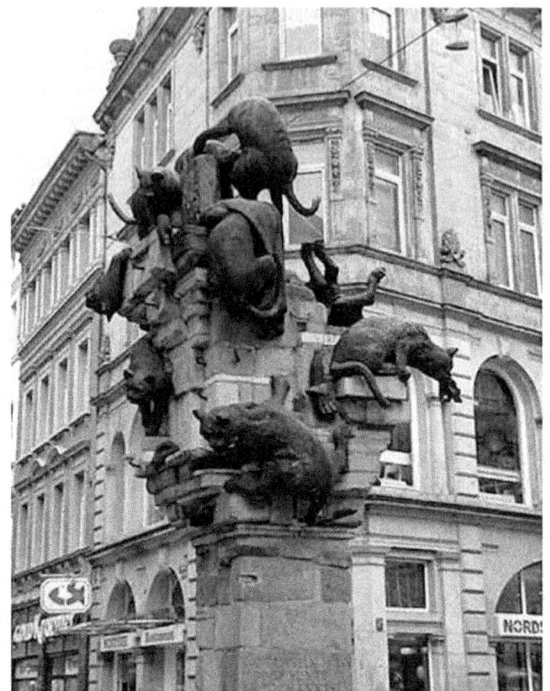

Памятник бездомным котам, Брауншвейг, Нижняя Саксония, Германия.

The Monument to the *"Homeless Cats"* is one of the most numerous on animals, established in Germany in Lower Saxony, the city of Braunschweig. There are many monuments to cats around the world, but this one attracts with its reality. People who were near the stele dedicated to homeless cats, note that they waited, when at least one of the cats is crammed.

Million dollars cat

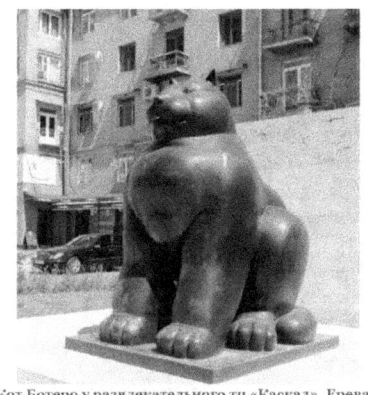

Кот Ботеро у развлекательного тц «Каскад», Ереван, Армения.

Perhaps, the most expensive monument to a cat is in **Yerevan**. This is one of three works devoted to cats by the famous sculptor Fernando Botero.

In 2002, the family Gafezchanov gave this monument to the city. It is worth one million dollars.

***

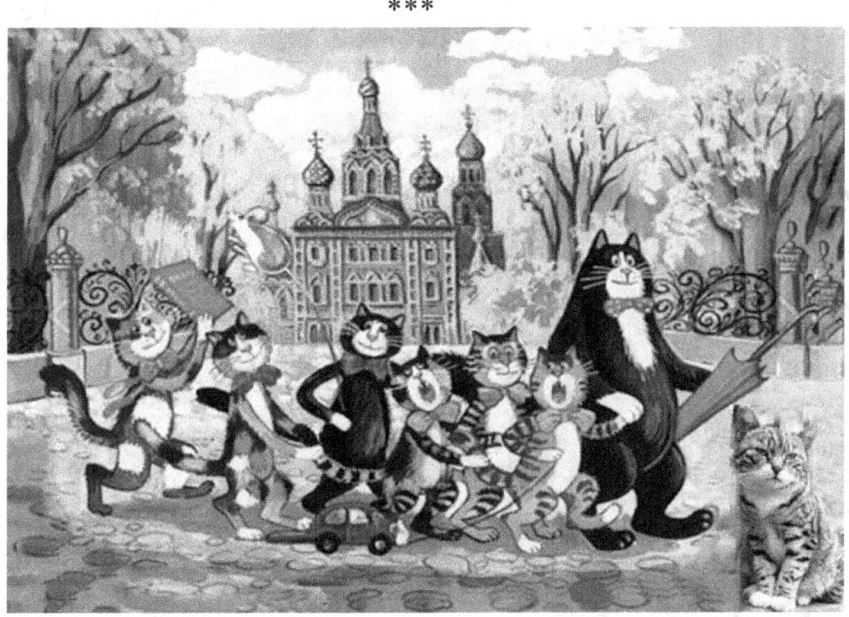

Around the Globe

In many cities of the world there are monuments to cats that have benefited society. In **America**, on the banks of the Mississippi River, a cat from the famous book of Mark Twain "*The Adventures of Tom Soare*" is immortalized. This is the same dead cat, with the help of which Huck and Tom were going to get rid of the warts. The sculpture depicts two boys who hold the tail of a dead cat.

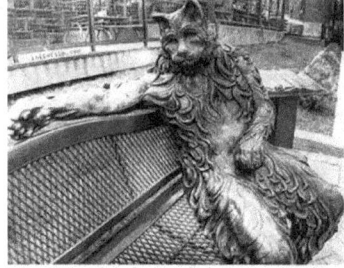
Скульптура Кот на скамейке, Мэриленд, США.

In **Paris**, before the University of the Sorbonne, there is a monument to cats who at the cost of life helped scientists conduct research in the field of physiology.

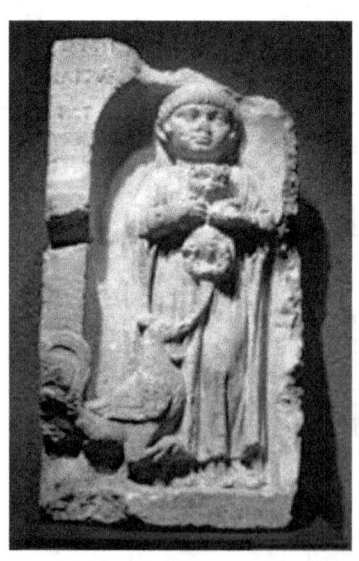

Until now, one of the oldest monuments to cats in the city of **Bordeaux**, in the South of France, has been preserved. The cat accompanied the conquering Roman legions not only on banners, but also physically. The Tombstone of Laetus's daughter, now in the Museum of Bordeaux, stands as a fine representation of the spread of Roman culture, and we see that young children along with their pets and toys were often forever memorialized on fureral steles and tombstones.

On the tombstone stands a young girl, holding her pet cat and a rooster at her side (Laetu's Daughter. 2nd Century AD. Musee d"Acquitane, Bordeaux). This is a well-known tombstone of a young

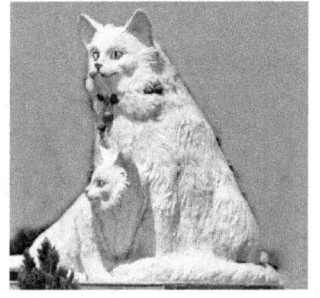

girl who died about 2000 years ago. Despite the antiquity, the image of the girl is well preserved. The girl is shown in full growth, and on hands she holds a cat, and not in the most convenient for it pose.

In **Turkey**, on the biggest lake of the country - Van, there is a monument to the cats of the breed "*Turkish Van*". This rare and beautiful breed of cats brought glory to its homeland, for which it was immortalized. Cats of the breed Turkish Van, in spite of many of their brethren, are not afraid of water and do not mind swim.

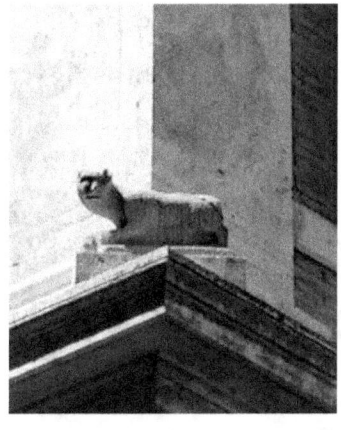

In **Rome**, a whole street is known and named after the cat - *Via della Gatta*. On one of the houses there is a sculpture of a marble cat. Once it was found near the Temple of Isis and installed on the cornice of the building Grazioli. According to another version, the cat was awarded a monument for the rescue of the child. The kid, who was unattended, climbed onto the cornice and nearly fell out of the window. The cat, noticing the child, raised a cry, than attracted the attention of the mother, who at the last moment had time to grab her child.

In **Australia**, in Sydney, there is a monument to the cat Trima - the pet of Captain Matthew Flinders. This cat is famous for being the first of all sorts to enter the land of the Australian continent. The captain and the command of the English military ship "Confidence" valued their black and white paws with a ship's cat. Once the cat, to the horror of the whole crew, fell overboard, but did not go to the bottom. He managed to swim to the ship and scramble aboard by a rope hanging from the side. In the city of **Resenburg** there is a monument to a cat, which is considered a monument to the cat Cheshire - it's a painful smile. And what a monument means in fact, just like no one knows.

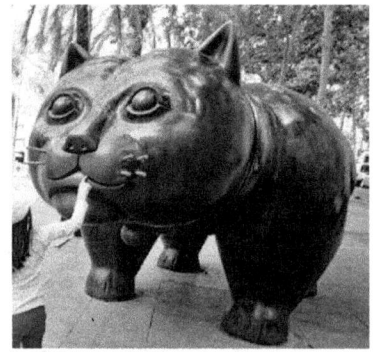

In **Latvia,** in the city of Klaipeda, there is a monument to a walking cat. The cat's face clearly shows the features of a man's face. According to rumors, the tail of this cat should be rubbed by a woman who wants to become pregnant.

Our Wonderful Cats

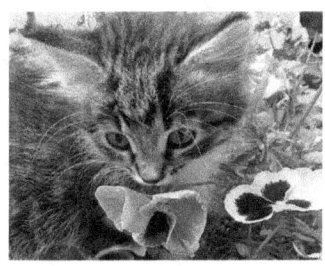

Many experts from different countries believe that cats are a real cure for heart disease, stress and even drunkenness. But most importantly, cats teach us how to be ourselves, to learn independence and *"to land on the feet, from where life would not shed"*. So we should not be shy about hooting and photographing our pets, sharing the joy of their love with friends. This, as scientists say, strengthens the nerves and helps to survive stress. When it is a difficult day, you must certainly stroke the cat. The murmur of our favorite fuzzy, as scientists from the University of Toronto (Canada) have established, activates in the human brain the same pleasure centers that delicious food or alcohol. Among pet owners, especially cats, there are far fewer alcoholics than among single people.

It is also important to know that cats save from cardiac catastrophes. Scientists from Scotland have established a link between the state of human health and the presence of pets. The owners of cats on average by 18-20% less often became victims of heart attacks or strokes. Experts say that cats reduce the risk of cancer and prolong the life of a strong sex. In any case, among those who lived to the age of 85 in the UK, more than 70% always kept at home cats.

Researchers from the department of oncological diseases at Stanford University in San Francisco spent seven years monitoring several thousand visitors to city polyclinics. It turned out that among those who indicated the presence of pets (cats and dogs) in the questionnaire for seven years, cancer fell on 30% fewer people than among those who did not keep pets.

Cats are our home physiotherapists and live "mustard plasters." Smoothing cats is very useful for all hypertensives and meteosensitive people (if there is no allergy). It is proved: stroking a cat's fur reduces blood pressure. This effect is achieved due to the removal of static electricity, and as a result, relieve tension and spasms of small vessels - the capillaries.

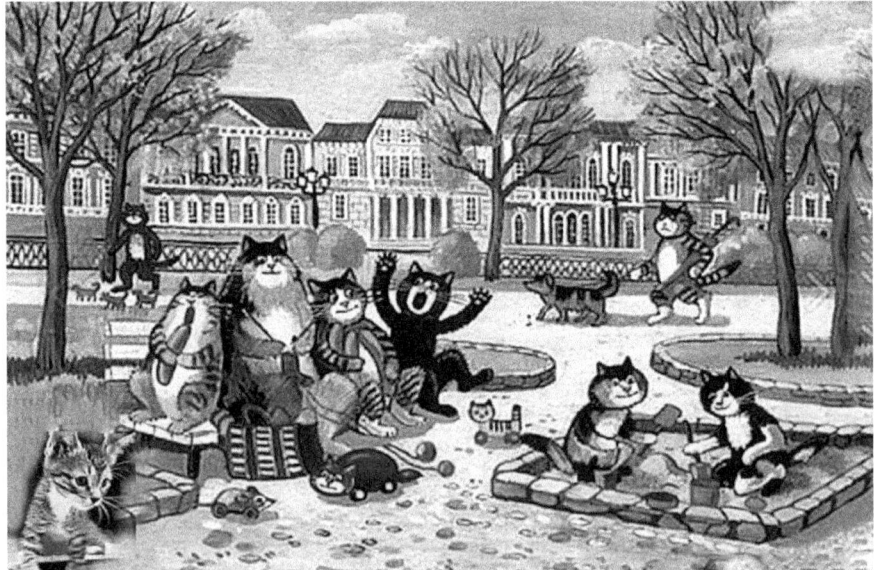

Cats very accurately distinguish the temperature difference even in half a degree. They love to bask and instinctively try to get settled in the warmest place. That is why if, for example, you have a knee joint inflammation or a bronchitis that starts, the cat will gladly climb either on its legs or on its chest. Living heat very effectively soothes this kind of pain and helps fight inflammation. So if you have the flu, and the cat decided to play a "live yellow card", do not throw it away, let it sit for a couple of minutes in a sore spot, and it will just become easier for you.

***

Our cats are so wonderful creatures. People continue to love them and make the masterpieaces, like in the drawings of Tatyana Radionova (St.Petersburg), as well as putting more monuments to the cats around the world.

***

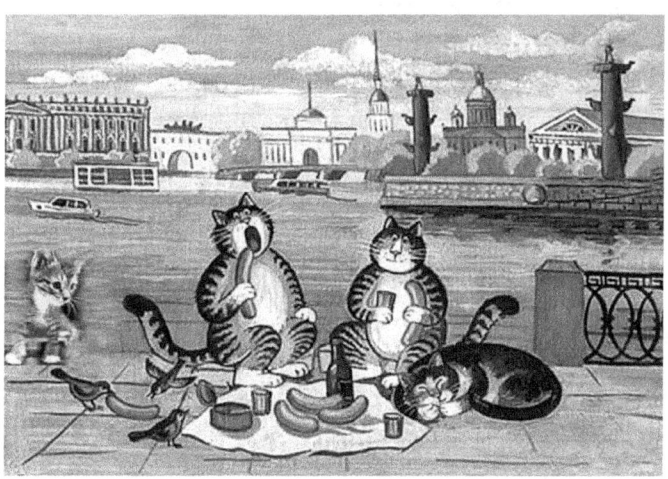

About Author

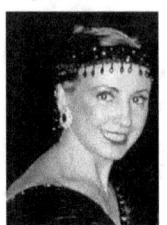

Elena Pankey is the author of several fun books about Argentine Tango dancing, art, and adventures.

She has Russian-Greek heritage, graduated from the prestigious Leningrad State University as a philologist-linguist. She has more than 45 years of job experience in different areas. During 1980's and 1990's she worked as a sound assistant of the movie productions, radio journalist, newspaper correspondent, tour guide, owned a businesses, and traveled the world. Also, she studied different dance styles and movements, including Mexican, African, Russian and authentic Gypsy dance, music (accordion), and acting skills. People called her "Twinkles Feet", "Queen of Tango," "Tango Icon".

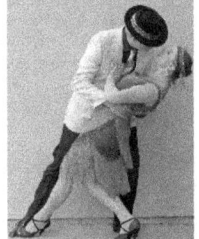

Elena has been married for more than 20 years and while living in CA, continues to travel the world, teaching, dancing and writing. She developed a tango course which has helps people improve the quality of their lives and marriages.

***

New books: www.TangoCaminito.com

www.ingramcontent.com/pod-product-compliance
Lightning Source LLC
Chambersburg PA
CBHW050027230526
45470CB00003B/1168